On the WING

North American Birds 6

Andrea Voon   Richard Han

← 42-62 cm →

Pied-billed Grebe

French: Grèbe à bec bigarré

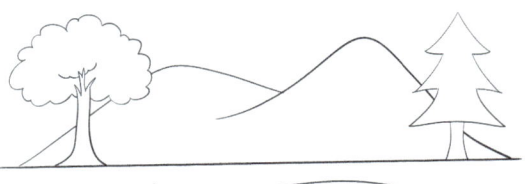

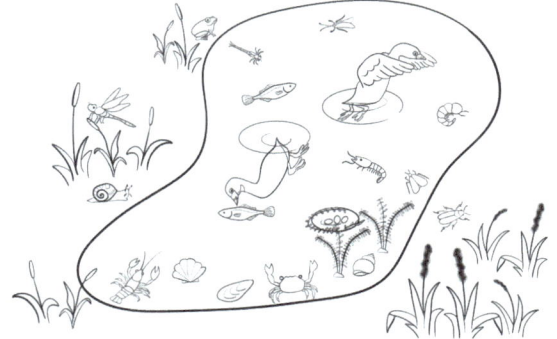

Great big wings, great big wings, flap flap flap…

Houseboat residents in the lakes and ponds are on the wing.

Pied-billed Grebes, Pied-billed Grebes, clap clap clap…

Build their floating nests in the spring.

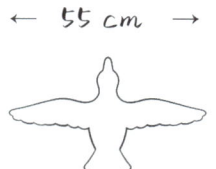

← 55 cm →

Bufflehead

French: Petit Garrot

Great big wings, great big wings, flap flap flap…

Hip-hop singers in the lakes and ponds are on the wing.

Buffleheads, buffleheads, clap clap clap…

Bob their head and rock their wing in the spring.

4

← 56-62 cm →

Ruddy Duck

French: Érismature rousse

Great big wings, great big wings, flap flap flap...

Comedy actors in the marshes are on the wing.

Ruddy Ducks, Ruddy Ducks, clap clap clap...

Perform their silly courtship in the spring.

← 56 - 66 cm →

Harlequin Duck

French: Arlequin plongeur

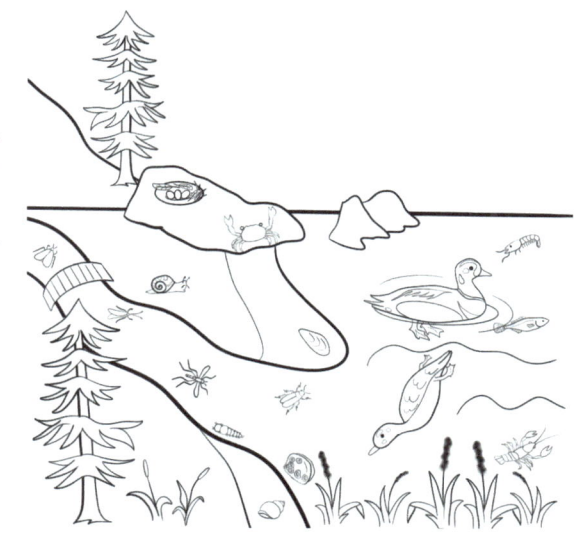

Great big wings, great big wings, flap flap flap...

Clowns in the rivers and streams are on the wing.

Harlequin Ducks, Harlequin Ducks, clap clap clap...

Surf on the rough water in the spring.

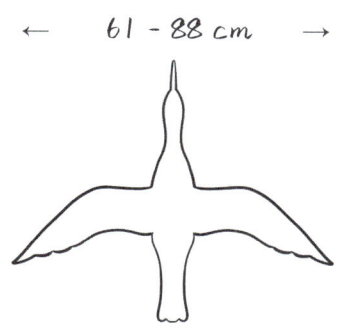

← 61 - 88 cm →

Red-necked Grebe

French: Grèbe jougris

Great big wings, great big wings, flap flap flap...

Bullfighters in the lakes and ponds are on the wing.

Red-necked Grebes, Red-necked Grebes, clap clap clap...

Thrust their bill, and hunch forward in the spring.

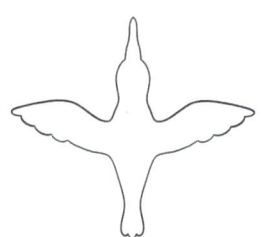

← 60 - 66 cm →

Hooded Merganser

French: Harle couronné

Great big wings, great big wings, flap flap flap…

Hairstylists in the lakes and ponds are on the wing.

Hooded Mergansers, Hooded Mergansers, clap clap clap…

Hunt with their special 'goggles' in the spring.

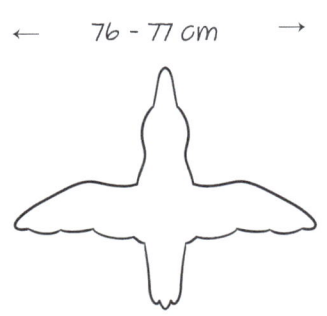

← 76 - 77 cm →

Surf Scoter

French: Macreuse à front blanc

Great big wings, great big wings, flap flap flap...

Surfers in the oceans are on the wing.

Surf Scoters, Surf Scoters, clap clap clap...

Form a large flock in the spring.

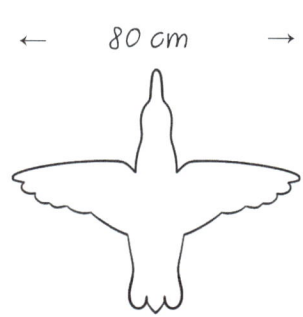

← 80 cm →

White-winged Scoter

French: Macreuse à ailes blanches

Great big wings, great big wings, flap flap flap…

Cruise ship passengers in the lakes and ponds are on the wing.

White-winged Scoters, white-winged Scoters, clap clap clap…

Show up on inland lakes in the spring.

← 69 - 84 cm →

Northern Shoveler

French: Canard souchet

Great big wings, great big wings, flap flap flap…

Lute players in the marshes are on the wing.

Northern Shovelers, Northern Shovelers, clap clap clap…

Sweep their bills to filter food in the spring.

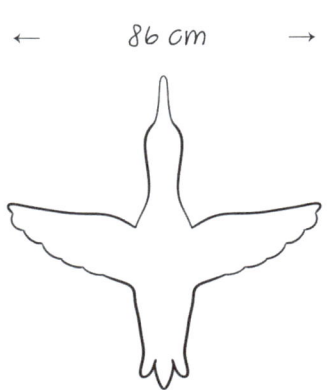

← 86 cm →

Common Merganser

French: Grand Harle

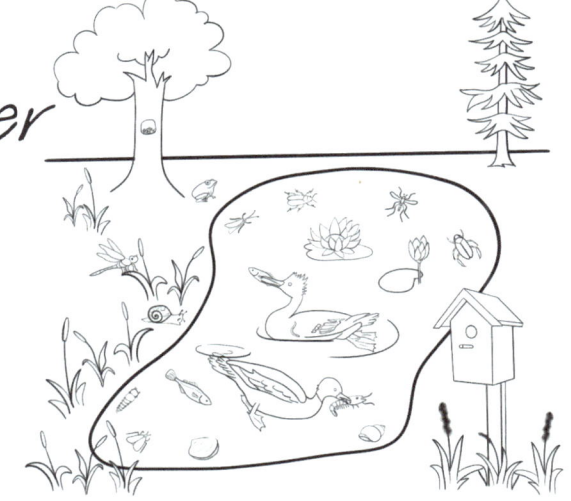

Great big wings, great big wings, flap flap flap...

Lumberjacks in the lakes and ponds are on the wing.

Common Mergansers, Common Mergansers, clap clap clap...

Hunt with their serrated bill in the spring.

Brant

French: Bernache cravant

Great big wings, great big wings, flap flap flap…

Golfers in the marshes are on the wing.

Brants, Brants, clap clap clap…

Feed heavily on eelgrass in the spring.

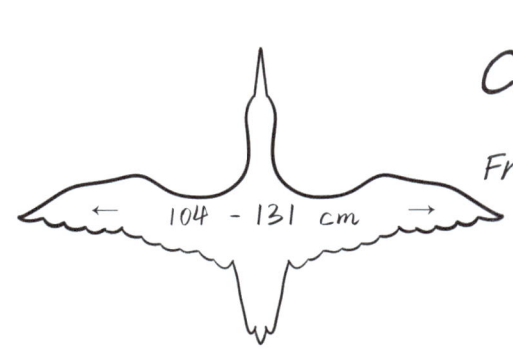

Common Loon

French: Plongeon huard

104 - 131 cm

Great big wings, great big wings, flap flap flap...

Submariners in the lakes and ponds are on the wing.

Common Loons, Common Loons, clap clap clap...

Expel air to dive and swim in the spring.

Snow Goose

French: Oie des neiges

138 cm

Great big wings, great big wings, flap flap flap...

Aquathlon athletes in the lakes and ponds are on the wing.

Snow Geese, Snow Geese, clap clap clap...

Fly, walk, and swim together in the spring.

Waterfowl, waterfowl, flap flap flap...

Travel to their breeding ground on the wing.

Seasonal partners, lifelong partners, clap clap clap...

Prepare for the breeding season in the spring.

Author

Andrea Voon

Over the past few years, Andrea has learned and grown with her family as a full-time mother in Canada. Back in Malaysia, she was a Chinese immersion elementary school teacher. In 2021, Andrea started her journey as an author. Growing up in a multilingual environment, Andrea loves the beauty of languages on their own. She has the vision to publish picture books to support bilingual families in raising their children in English, Chinese, and Cantonese reading.

Photographer

Richard Han

Richard loves to practice patience through his lenses of the natural world. He enjoys observing the wildlife and photographing the natural lifestyles that animals live. He is excited to present the beautiful photos that he captured in dreamy tones and colors to all the birds lover.

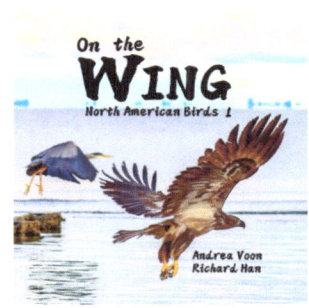

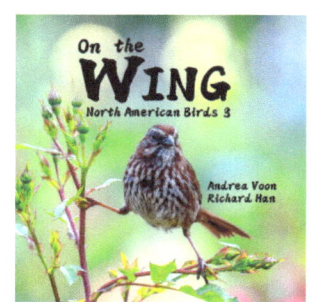

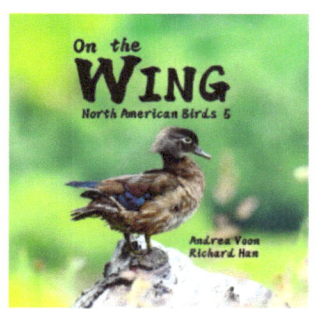

To **Shirley Han, Derek, Eliana, Alayna & Magnus Dominus**

with love -- Andrea. V

For **Richard Han**

The patience in natural photography

ISBN 978-1-998856-54-1
Text Copyright © 2024 Andrea Voon
Photo Credit © 2024 Richard Han